IF you're reading this, you're our kind of motherfucker. Or you just might be a fan of Dare You Stamp Co. already. And why wouldn't you be? We're awesome. Our line of completely irreverent products is perfect for sticking it to the man and flipping off your haters with style.

Whether you signed your vacation request with our *F This Shit Stamp Kit*, told Santa where he can shove his coal with our *Tis the Season to Be Naughty Postcards*, or became the antihero of your dreams with our *POW! Stamp Kit*, you know we're done being polite. So why not tell the world to fuck off? Break out that pack of colored pencils that you abandoned in middle school and connect the fucking dots! Frame them, hang them, or leave them all over your boss's desk with your resignation letter stapled to the back. What you do with these are up to you, dumbass. If you feel like showing off, you can share your fucking awesome creations with the hashtag #fuckoffimdoingdottodot.

Now go forth and be the complete asshole you were meant to be, we dare you.

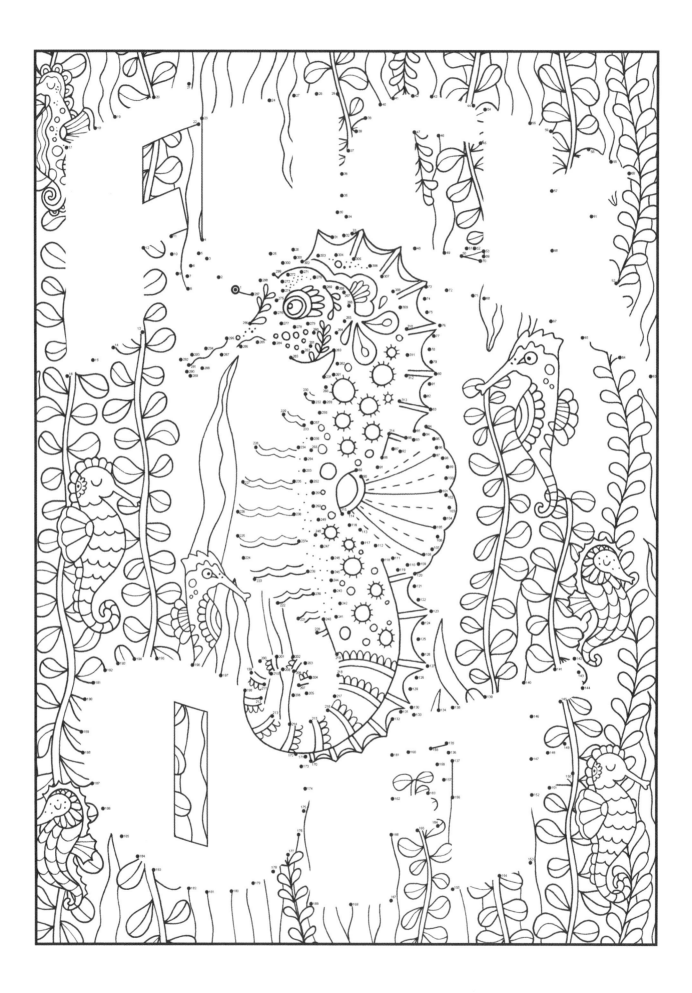

TABLE of CONTENTS

INTRODUCTION 7

WORDS TO LIVE BY
Connect the dots, dammit! 8

#GOALS
Aim high, hero. 26

TELL IT LIKE IT IS
Embrace the truth. 42

SAY IT LOUD
Make sure everyone knows how you feel. 64

PROFANE SELF-CARE
Being dignified is overrated. 90

INTRODUCTION

You know how therapists tell you to take a deep breath and count to ten when the world seems out to get you and you want to scream at the top of your lungs? Well, that might work for some folks, but fuck that shit.

Sometimes you need to let the anger out. What better way to vent pent-up rage than counting way past ten, and watching the anger inside take shape outside of you in these curse-filled, edgy dot-to-dot pages?

Shitty boss? Bad drivers? Annoying family? Needy friends? Channel all of that bullshit into these pages.

Do it now, dammit!

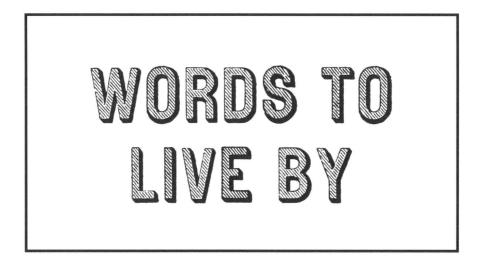

WORDS TO
LIVE BY

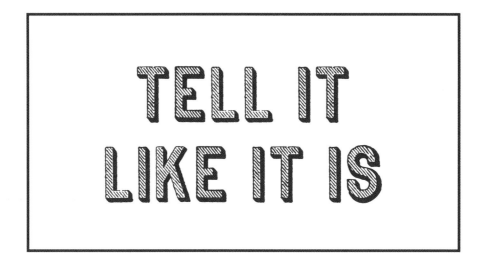

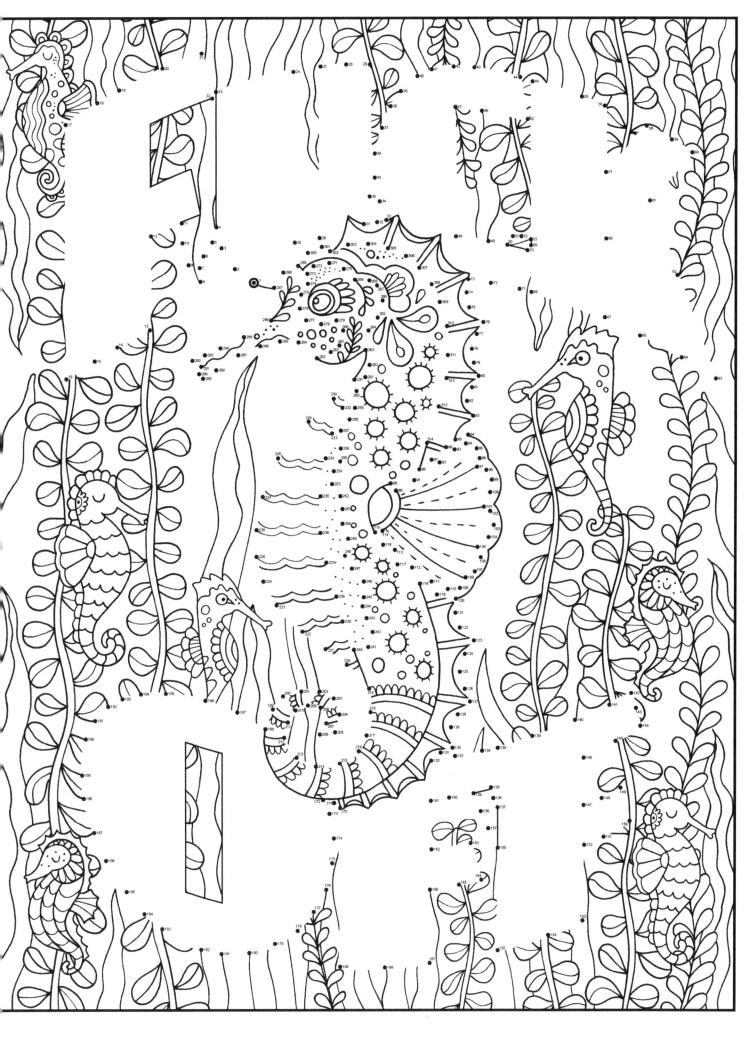

PROFANE
SELF-CARE

#FUCKOFFIMDOINGDOTTODOT #FUCKOFFIMDOINGDOTTODOT
#FUCKOFFIMDOINGDOTTODOT #FUCKOFFIMDOINGDOTTODOT
#FUCKOFFIMDOINGDOTTODOT #FUCKOFFIMDOINGDOTTODOT
#FUCKOFFIMDOINGDOTTODOT #FUCKOFFIMDOINGDOTTODOT
#FUCKOFFIMDOINGDOTTODOT #FUCKOFFIMDOINGDOTTODOT
#FUCKOFFIMDOINGDOTTODOT #FUCKOFFIMDOINGDOTTODOT
#FUCKOFFIMDOINGDOTTODOT #FUCKOFFIMDOINGDOTTODOT
#FUCKOFFIMDOINGDOTTODOT #FUCKOFFIMDOINGDOTTODOT
#FUCKOFFIMDOINGDOTTODOT #FUCKOFFIMDOINGDOTTODOT
#FUCKOFFIMDOINGDOTTODOT #FUCKOFFIMDOINGDOTTODOT
#FUCKOFFIMDOINGDOTTODOT #FUCKOFFIMDOINGDOTTODOT
#FUCKOFFIMDOINGDOTTODOT #FUCKOFFIMDOINGDOTTODOT
#FUCKOFFIMDOINGDOTTODOT #FUCKOFFIMDOINGDOTTODOT
#FUCKOFFIMDOINGDOTTODOT #FUCKOFFIMDOINGDOTTODOT
#FUCKOFFIMDOINGDOTTODOT #FUCKOFFIMDOINGDOTTODOT
#FUCKOFFIMDOINGDOTTODOT #FUCKOFFIMDOINGDOTTODOT
#FUCKOFFIMDOINGDOTTODOT #FUCKOFFIMDOINGDOTTODOT
#FUCKOFFIMDOINGDOTTODOT #FUCKOFFIMDOINGDOTTODOT
#FUCKOFFIMDOINGDOTTODOT #FUCKOFFIMDOINGDOTTODOT
#FUCKOFFIMDOINGDOTTODOT #FUCKOFFIMDOINGDOTTODOT
#FUCKOFFIMDOINGDOTTODOT #FUCKOFFIMDOINGDOTTODOT
#FUCKOFFIMDOINGDOTTODOT #FUCKOFFIMDOINGDOTTODOT
#FUCKOFFIMDOINGDOTTODOT #FUCKOFFIMDOINGDOTTODOT
#FUCKOFFIMDOINGDOTTODOT #FUCKOFFIMDOINGDOTTODOT

SHARE YOUR BITCHIN' MASTERPIECES

Don't keep your colorful creations
to yourself—take a pic and share it
on social media with the hashtag
#fuckoffimdoingdottodot!

For more stress-relieving coloring, check out:
Fuck Off, I'm Coloring
Fuck Off, I'm Still Coloring
Fuck Off, I Can't Stop Coloring
Fuck Off, Coronavirus, I'm Coloring
Bite Me, I'm Coloring
Fuck Off, I'm Adorable
Fuck Off, Holidays, I'm Coloring
Available now!

INDEX

#

#IDGAF… 47
#STFU… 45

A

Adult as Fuck… 91
Asswipe… 75

B

Back Off… 49
Be Badass… 33
Bitch, Please… 69
Bite Me… 83
Buh-Bye… 103

C

Can You Not?… 15
Cheers to Me… 19

D

Day Drinking… 31
Dipshit… 77
Don't Be an Ass… 9

Don't Be a Prick… 25
Don't Kill My Vibe… 21

E

Epic… 35

F

For Fuck's Sake… 59
Fucking Hell… 79
Fuck Off… 81
Fuck That Noise… 61
Fuckwad… 57
Fuck Yeah… 107
Fuck You… 87

G

Get Out of My Face… 85
Grow a Pair… 63

H

Hella Fine!… 51
Hell Nah… 27
Hot Mess… 89

I

I Just Can't... 17

K

Killin' It!... 37

L

Legend... 41

N

Nasty... 97
No Fucks Given... 43
No One Cares... 71
Nope... 11
Not Today... 23

O

Over It... 13

R

Respect... 39

S

Screw It... 105
See You Never... 101
Seriously?... 53
Shit Show... 67
Sit and Spin... 55
Sorry Not Sorry... 95

T

Tired & Wired... 93

U

UGH... 73

Y

You're the Tits... 99
You Suck... 65

Z

Zen as Fuck... 29

ABOUT
DARE YOU STAMP CO.

Dare You Stamp Co. was founded in 1776 when noted Philadelphian Jeremiah Dare was hired by the not-yet-Founding Fathers to print draft copies of the Declaration of Independence.

When the documents arrived at Independence Hall, an unfortunate typo read "When in the Curse of human events…"

So irate was George Washington that he said, "The foolish and wicked practice of profane cursing and swearing is a vice so mean and low that every person of sense and character detests and despises it."

Dare's instinct was to simply reply, "Fuck you."